A story by Lori Henninger Smith

Down by the Dock

The adventures of an Irish dolphin named Finn
and how he came to be in Carlingford Lough, now and again.

Illustrations by Alice Pescarin

ISBN: 978-1-7379407-3-9

Down by the Dock
Library of Congress Control Number: 2021923193

Silver Girl Sails Publishing, Ltd.
Little Rock, AR USA

A story by Lori Henninger Smith
Illustrations by Alice Pescarin

www.finnandfungiebooks.com

I dedicate this book to my grandkids: Jackson, Bella, Dawson, Hudson and Emmerson (Emme). I want you to always know it's never too late to go after your dreams and live a life you love.

SCAN AND LISTEN

TO BEGIN LISTENING TO THIS BOOK, SCAN THIS CODE. TURN THE PAGE WHEN YOU HEAR THE DOLPHIN SQUEAK! HAVE FUN!

Little dolphin,
where did you come from?

Where have
you been?

Will you be coming
around again?

In the beautiful waters of Carlingford Lough,
a new visitor was spotted down by the dock.
It was a dolphin, very rare in these parts.
The kids were delighted; it warmed their hearts.

But the people of Carlingford Lough wanted to know,

"Who is this new friend?
How can we say hello?"

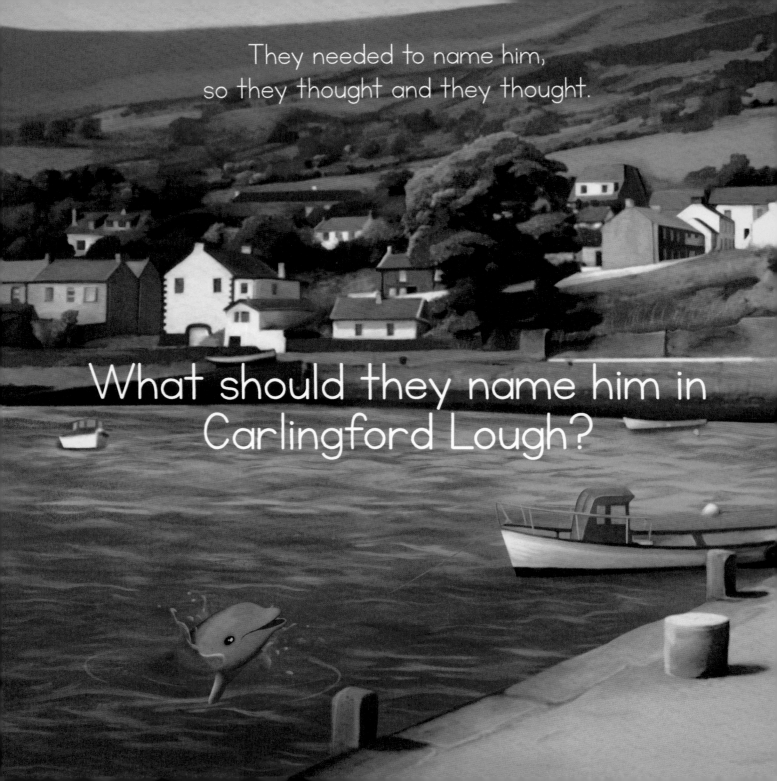

They needed to name him,
so they thought and they thought.

What should they name him in
Carlingford Lough?

They took a poll and choose the name

"Finn"

and that new name made everyone grin.

SCAN AND LEARN

Now their next question was,

"Finn, where are you from?"

Dolphins were rare in the area, so their brains were numb!

How did a dolphin arrive in their town?

Not many had ever been seen around.

They set off to determine from where Finn did arrive.
They wanted to make sure he continued to thrive.

Finn loved to play by the ferry boat.

Did he catch a ride to stay afloat?

No, that's probably not right.

Not on a boat, **but maybe a kite!**

So the town pondered the theory
he came in on a kite.
But again, they determined that was probably not right.

SCAN AND LEARN

There's a rainbow almost every day in Ireland.

Could Finn have slid down one with an entrance so grand?

They've never seen a dolphin slide down a rainbow.

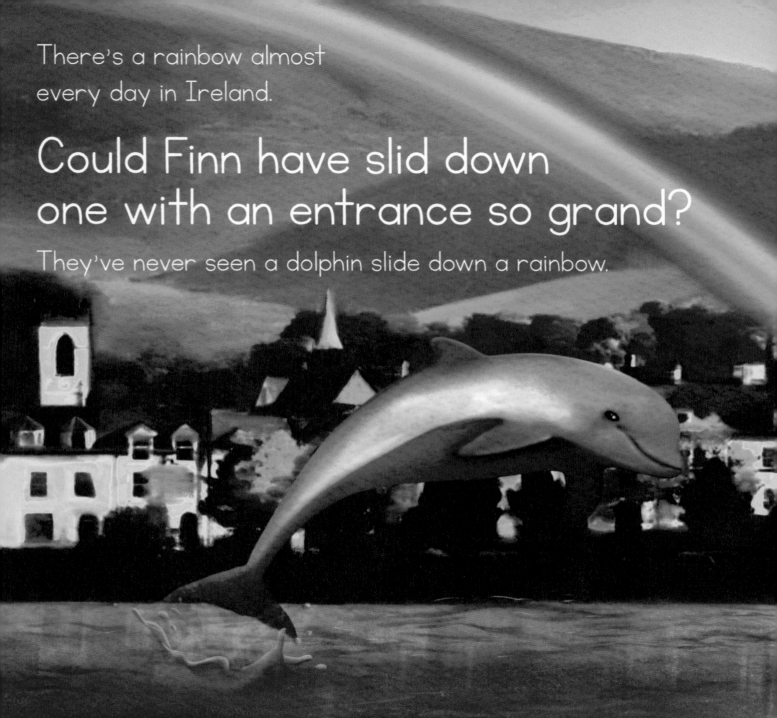

SCAN AND LEARN

But boy!
Wouldn't that be a fantastic show?

Once again, probably not.
But, that is a really neat thought!

In Ireland, there are many fables about giants.
They are great stories to hear and hard to keep silent.

Maybe a giant had a pet dolphin in a

goldfish bowl.

And, he slipped when his foot fell into a hole.

As he fell, the dolphin went flying through the air.

He flew up, up, up, and out of the giant's lair.

He flew in the air so high and so far,

he might have looked like a shooting star!

Then he fell in the waters of Carlingford Lough.
The people around were in a state of shock.
The waters broke his fall,
and he was happy to be there.
He was touched to see how much the people cared.

SCAN AND LEARN

He looked funny jumping and splashing around,
but it seemed there was something holding him down.

Some scuba divers went to check on Finn.

They removed some plastic,
so he could swim.

Once that was done, he splashed with glee, as if saying,

"Thank you for hearing my plea!"

There's a **lesson** here that everyone should learn.

You have a choice;

please take your turn.

Don't let your rubbish
get into the ocean.

Save dolphins and creatures;
it's more than a notion!

Rubbish can hurt animals big and small.
We want them to be safe and happy overall.

It's better to throw your trash into a bin.
And when you do, you can think about Finn,
the dolphin who lives in Carlingford Lough,

making everyone smile
down by the dock.

Meet the real Finn

2 Tanks Photography

©2TanksPhotography.ie

Finn is a bottlenosed dolphin who arrived in Carlingford around May of 2020, mainly staying around the ferry boat in Greenore. He has claimed this area as his home and we hope he stays a long time!

Divers John Kelly and Damian Smith check on him from time to time and have taken some great photos of him. Although he has adjusted to them being there, the ocean is his habitat and humans need to respect that it is his home, and give him the space he requires.

Dolphins are a protected species in both Ireland and the United States and all care needs to be given to ensure they are safe at all times.

Damian and John do just that. Here's what they said about being around Finn:

John: "To have this amazing opportunity to dive with a wild animal is just out of this world. Finn is very curious and when I look into his eyes, it's like there is a trust there. I may be superstitious here, my diving buddy Anthony of 12 years passed away in Jan. 2020. I can't help in wondering if Anthony sent him to us. We are very lucky to have Finn appear when he wants."

Damian: "I always dreamed of diving with dolphins. Being up close and personal with such a large wild dolphin is a humbling experience. When Finn comes within inches of me and looks into my eyes, it's easy to see the intelligence, curiosity and personality that he has. Finn doesn't always show up when we dive, but when he does show up, it's always on his terms."

I had requested photos of Finn for this book and Aaron Treanor offered this one of Finn surfacing. Aaron is a 17 year old aspiring photographer in the area. This picture of Finn was his first shot of wildlife after photographing planes at the Dublin airport. Thank you, Aaron, for contributing to our book about Finn!

# of Carlingford Lough!

Did **you** know?

Did you know this book turns into an audio book by scanning the code on the dedication page? You can listen as Irish Folksinger Orla Travers narrates the book for you! That's fun when you're tired and still want to hear a story at bedtime!

SCAN AND LEARN

Did you know you can scan these codes through-out the books to learn more about dolphins or castles or other things in the book? And those lessons will change from time to time! So next time, you may learn something new!

Did you know you are helping to free whales and dolphins around the world by reading this book? A portion of all proceeds goes to Marine Connection to help captive whales and dolphins retire to seaside sanctuaries. www.marineconnection.org

Did you know we have a website with fun stuff to do? You can get colouring sheets, and lesson plans for teachers and watch videos of Finn and Fungie and much more! Be sure to check it out!

www.finnandfungiebooks.com

Did you know you can help us tell other people about the books by writing a review on Amazon? Your review will help us raise money for Marine Connection to help more dolphins! Be sure to go to Amazon to write a review! We appreciate it so much!

Finn and Fungie want to thank you for helping them help other dolphins and whales live freely as they are meant to! They are so happy to have you on their team!

Thank you for your review!

Thank you Carlingford and Dingle and all of Ireland and the world! We love you, Too! Signed, Finn and Fungie

About these fun things?

Meet the Author

Lori Henninger Smith

I studied studio art and graphic design at the University of Arkansas at Little Rock, USA. After a long career in marketing and home decor product design, I crossed the Atlantic Ocean to return to college at the age of 57.

Always in love with Ireland, I chose to study Public Relations and Digital Marketing Communications. With the encouragement of my creative writing lecturer, Ciara, I found my purpose. From my home on the waters of Carlingford Lough, (pronounced 'lock' for my American friends), I heard stories of a curious new and rare, dolphin in the area and began to imagine where this dolphin came from. Always enthralled by the folklore, myths and legends in Ireland that include giants, I could imagine a story evolving I knew my grandkids would enjoy. And "Down by the Dock" was born.

Then a friend mentioned the story of Fungie and after much research, "Finn's Friend Fungie" became a reality as well. Both books have been well received and we hope you enjoy them, too!

Thank you, Finn and Fungie, for helping me discover my passion.

Alice Pescarin

I have a degree in advertising and graphics, a graduate in communication psychology at the University of Milan-Bicocca and a degree in design and illustration from the IED in Milan.

My experience began during my school years, working as an art director and graphic designer in the field of advertising and e-commerce and following my passion for illustration, which has become my main occupation.

I use mixed, manual and digital techniques.

Currently, I live and work in Grosseto – ITALY, as an illustrator of children's books, collaborating with publishers mainly in the USA and with international authors, supporting the realization of their literary projects.

Meet the Illustrator

Check out Fungie's book!

We hope you liked reading this story about Finn.
Finn wants you to know about his friend Fungie in Dingle Bay. You can read about him next in his very own book called Finn's Friend Fungie!

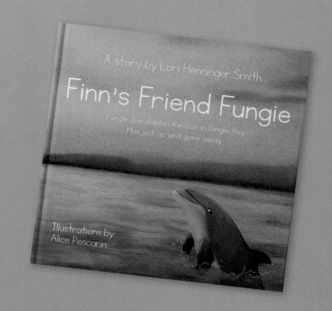

A story by Lori Henninger Smith

Finn's Friend Fungie

Fungie the dolphin famous in Dingle Bay
Has just up and gone away.

Illustrations by
Alice Pescarin

Thank you!

SCAN AND LISTEN

Printed in Great Britain
by Amazon